# THE
# STAFFORDSHIRE
# MOORLANDS

## Volume 2

A Portrait in Old Picture Postcards

by
George Bowyer and Ray Poole

Brampton Publications
1989

First published in 1989 by Brampton Publications.

℅ 5 Queen Margaret's Road, Loggerheads, Nr. Market Drayton, Shropshire, TF9 4EP.

© Copyright 1989 Brampton Publications.

All rights reserved.

ISBN 1 871528 04 6

Printed in Great Britain by Rubell Print Ltd., Bunbury, Tarporley, Cheshire, CW6 9PQ.

Bound by J W Braithwaite and Son Limited, Pountney Street, Wolverhampton WV2 4HY.

# CONTENTS

|  | Page |
|---|---|
| Introduction | |
| BIDDULPH | 1 – 14 |
| KNYPERSLEY | 15 |
| BIDDULPH MOOR | 16 – 17 |
| BROWN EDGE | 18 |
| HORTON | 19 |
| SWYTHAMLEY | 20 |
| RUSHTON | 21 – 24 |
| RUDYARD | 25 – 26 |
| MEERBROOK | 27 – 28 |
| LEEK | 29 – 45 |
| BRADNOP | 46 |
| THORNCLIFFE | 47 |
| UPPERHULME | 48 |
| LONGSDON | 49 – 50 |
| WALL GRANGE | 51 – 52 |
| ENDON | 53 – 60 |
| BAGNALL | 61 |
| LEEKBROOK | 62 – 64 |
| CHEDDLETON | 65 – 70 |
| WETLEY ROCKS | 71 – 72 |
| CONSALL | 73 – 75 |
| FROGHALL | 76 – 77 |

# CONTENTS CONTINUED

| | Page |
|---|---|
| CAULDON | 78 |
| CALDON LOW | 79 – 80 |
| WATERHOUSES | 81 – 83 |
| FORD | 84 |
| MANIFOLD VALLEY | 85 – 89 |
| WETTON MILL | 90 |
| ECTON | 91 – 93 |
| HULME END | 94 – 95 |
| SHEEN | 96 |
| BUTTERTON | 97 – 98 |
| ALSTONFIELD | 99 – 101 |
| HOLLINSCLOUGH | 102 |
| LONGNOR | 103 – 106 |
| WARSLOW | 107 – 108 |
| FLASH | 109 |
| LOWE HILL | 110 |
| IPSTONES | 111 – 112 |
| ONECOTE | 113 – 114 |
| ILAM | 115 – 118 |
| BERESFORD DALE | 119 |
| DOVE DALE | 120 |

Acknowledgements

Brampton Publications

# INTRODUCTION

The subject of this book is a pictorial representation in old picture postcards of the northern part of the Staffordshire Moorlands district, bounded in the south by the A52 Potteries to Ashbourne road. The sequence starts on the Cheshire border, and ends on the border with Derbyshire.

The main centres of population in the area are the towns of Biddulph and Leek, and the larger villages of Cheddleton, Ipstones and Endon. The area also includes large areas of open moorland, as wild, exposed and remote as any in the British Isles, dotted with isolated villages where time appears to have stood still for many years.

Agriculture has been a major industry of the area for centuries, but the industrialisation of certain parts of the moorlands is apparent in the remains of old mines, quarries and limekilns, linked by industrial plateways to the main arteries of trade and communication running through the area - the Caldon Canal and the Churnet Valley Railway.

We hope that this selection of old picture postcards, most of them hitherto unpublished except in their original form, will present a pictorial record of the life, history and topography of the area, whilst at the same time providing a worthy complement to George Short's first volume on the district, and reflect the changing and the changeless aspects of the Staffordshire Moorlands.

George Bowyer and Ray Poole
August, 1989

**BIDDULPH OLD HALL,** c. 1910

Biddulph Old Hall, built about 1558, was the home of the Biddulph family, Catholics, who supported the Royalist cause during the Civil War. In 1644 the hall was under siege from the Parliamentary army for about three months. Resistance collapsed in the face of superior forces, with cannons, and the garrison surrendered. Prisoners were taken and the destruction of the hall followed.

**OLD MILL, HURST ROAD, BIDDULPH**, c. 1905
A water-powered silk mill situated at the Hurst was shown on the Tithe Map dated 1840. At this time, three other silk mills were shown in the Biddulph area. White's Directory of 1851 lists Judith Harthan as a silk throwster at Hurst Mill.

*Parish Church and Schools, Biddulph.*

**PARISH CHURCH AND SCHOOLS, BIDDULPH,** c. 1918

The Parish Church of St. Lawrence, seen in this picture, retains a perpendicular north-west tower as well as early English arcades - otherwise it was rebuilt in 1833 to the designs of T. Trubshaw. There is an excellent 16th-century Flemish stained-glass window and numerous ornate monuments, notably to members of the Bowyer and Heath families. The church suffered damage during the Civil War. The schools, which also incorporated a Sunday School, were mentioned in a report of 1818.

**THE GRANGE, BIDDULPH,** c. 1895
This picture shows the original building before the disastrous fire of 1896 which destroyed the central block of the house. The outer wings were saved, and the centre was rebuilt by Robert Heath, who had purchased the Grange following the Bateman's retirement to Worthing. James Bateman died in 1897.

**THE GARDENS, BIDDULPH GRANGE,** c. 1910

The famous gardens at Biddulph Grange were the work of James Bateman, only son of John, who was born 1811. His great interest in botany began during his time at Magdalen College, Oxford, in 1829. Following his marriage in 1838 James and Maria Bateman lived at the Grange, where he settled permanently following the death of his father in 1858. The construction of the elaborate gardens then commenced.

**THE CHINESE GARDEN, BIDDULPH GRANGE,** c. 1910
The cleverly-concealed Chinese Garden to the east of the lake at Biddulph Grange is one of several spectacular creations. Other themes included the Egyptian Court (complete with stone sphinxes), the Cheshire Cottage, the Pinetum, the Arboretum, the Lime Walk, the Rhododendron-ground and the Wellingtonia Avenue.

THE GRANGE, BIDDULPH.

**THE GRANGE, BIDDULPH,** c. 1910

The Grange, showing the rebuilt central block and the tower added by Robert Heath following the fire of 1896. The Heaths left the Grange in 1922, and it was opened as a hospital by H.R.H. the Prince of Wales on 14th June 1924. It became an orthopeadic hospital under the Stoke-on-Trent Hospital Management Committee, and the grounds are now in the hands of the National Trust who have undertaken a large scheme to restore the gardens to their former glory.

**CONGLETON ROAD, BIDDULPH,** c. 1925

Congleton Road, which enters Biddulph from the north is now the busy A527 main road to the Potteries. The small shop on the left of the picture was a tea shop, serving refreshments. This postcard was produced by a local publisher - T. Whitehurst, printer and stationer - who had a shop in High Street, Biddulph.

**HIGH STREET, BIDDULPH,** c. 1920

The area formerly known as Bradley Green developed commercially during the second half of the 19th century to become the main shopping centre of Biddulph. The building on the extreme left was a post office, and the group of men are standing outside Baddiley's double-fronted shop. The shops on the right, leading up towards Wharf Road, have now been replaced by a modern supermarket. The picture was taken from the junction just outside the Royal Oak.

**BARBER'S PICTURE PALACE, BIDDULPH,** c. 1930
Cinematograph halls such as this imposing example sprang up in most towns with the growth in popularity of talking pictures. This building stood on the corner of King Street and John Street - the site now occupied by the Trustee Savings Bank.

*Hurst Towers, Biddulph.*

**HURST TOWERS, BIDDULPH,** c. 1920s
Situated on Hurst Road, this impressive residence with its Italianate tower, was the home in the 1920s - 30s of the town's surveyor and sanitary inspector, Shadrach Gibson.

**THE WAR MEMORIAL, BIDDULPH**
Unveiled in May 1922, this granite memorial with its marble figure of a First World War soldier was the work of a Biddulph man, Jonah Cottrell. This scene depicts a Royal visit to Biddulph when H.R.H. the Prince of Wales (later Duke of Windsor) laid a wreath on the cenotaph on 14th June 1924. It was a very rainy day, and the Prince also officially opened Biddulph Grange Hospital during his visit.

**BIDDULPH VALLEY IRONWORKS,** c. 1912

Initially agricultural, Biddulph developed from a group of villages which included Bradley Green, Gillow Heath, Knypersley and Brown Lees. The high northern boundary with Cheshire terminates in one direction by The Cloud, and in the other by Mow Cop. Biddulph developed as an industrial town during the 19th century, coal, ironstone and limestone were extensively worked, and there were textile and fustian mills. Biddulph Valley Ironworks, at Black Bull, were operated by Robert Heath, a notable ironmaster who came to Biddulph in 1857. In 1873 the works comprised 4 blast furnaces, as well as rolling mills and coal and ironstone pits.

**FOSSILIZED TREE TRUNK, BIDDULPH,** c. 1906

Inscribed on the metal band encircling this fossilized tree trunk is the following: "This Fossil was got out of the roof in the Holly Lane seam at a depth of 244 yards on 10th September 1906 at the Brown Lees Colliery, Biddulph, Staffordshire".

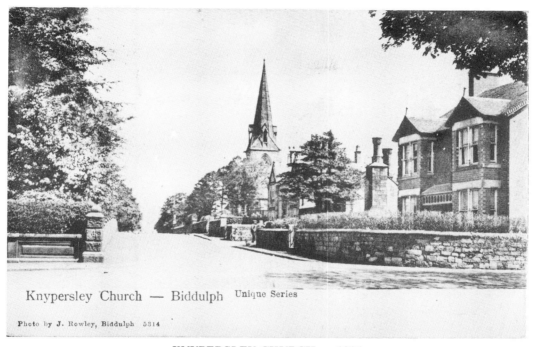

**KNYPERSLEY CHURCH,** c. 1904

The Church of St. John the Evangelist at Knypersley was built in 1848 - 51 by John Bateman of Biddulph Grange at a cost of £10,000. The large vicarage, with coach house and stables, and the nearby school in Newpool Road were also the gift of Mr. Bateman.

**BIDDULPH MOOR - THE ROAD TO THE HURST,** c. 1917
The gritty community still retains many of its old stone-built properties, now interspersed with more modern housing developments. It was formed as a separate ecclesiastical parish in 1864 from the parishes of Biddulph and Horton. Its proximity to Mow Cop meant that it was for many years a stronghold of Primitive Methodism.

SOURCE OF THE TRENT, BIDDULPH, nr. HANLEY.

**THE SOURCE OF THE TRENT,** c. 1906
The River Trent, which passes through many towns and cities along its 170-mile course before entering the North Sea, has its humble source in the Staffordshire Moorlands, near Biddulph Moor. The two persons portrayed in this turn-of-the-century picture are Thomas Plant and Mrs. Fanny Battersby. There is an old belief that the waters of the spring had medicinal qualities.

**BROWN EDGE HOCKEY CLUB,** 1912-13
A note on the reverse of the card states that 6 men are missing from the group, and that both men's and mixed matches were played.

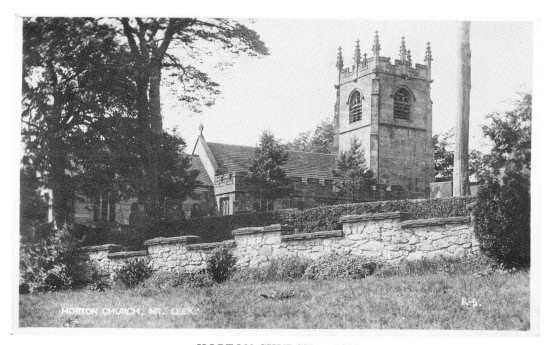

**HORTON CHURCH,** c. 1913

The early 17th-century St. Michael's Church, Horton contains some work by the Leek architect William Sugden - the south arcade and the east window. There are also several monuments to members of the Wedgwood family. In the churchyard, a large, elaborate cross marks the grave of George Heath, the Moorland poet, who lived at Gratton, and died 5th May 1869 aged 25 years. The cross was designed by his friend, H. W. Foster.

**SWYTHAMLEY CHURCH,** c. 1905
Swythamley Church is situated on the Swythamley Park estate. The small stone-built chapel with the rose window was built by the Brocklehursts in 1905. The church has a unique water-powered peel of bells.

**RUSHTON**, c. 1910

The main road from Leek to Macclesfield is seen here as it enters the village of Rushton. On the right is the Hanging Gate public house, which has an actual "hanging gate" as its inn sign. The road to Congleton (Beat Lane) is on the left, which passes Cloudside and the Bridestones, a Neolithic burial chamber.

Rushton, near Leek.

**RUSHTON,** c. 1905
In White's Directory of Staffordshire (1851) three Rushtons are mentioned: Rushton-James (1000 acres in the manor of Horton), Rushton-Spencer (1500 acres, including the Church of St. Lawrence) and Rushton-Marsh, where there were three public houses, a Methodist Chapel, a school (1772) and the railway station.

**RUSHTON,** c. 1905
This scene shows Sugar Street, near the school, with three villagers, left to right: Harriet Dale (later Mrs. Turnock), Postman Dale (her father) and Mrs. Moss.

**RUSHTON WELL-DRESSING,** 1907
The custom of well-dressing, usually associated with Derbyshire, had another "outpost" in the Moorlands area - at Rushton. The scene here is of the 1907 ceremony, with the Well-dressing Queen being carried aloft. The religious significance of these thanksgiving ceremonies is apparent as the men raise their hats as the vicar offers prayers. The well at Rushton was named St. Helen's Well and was located near to the Church of St. Lawrence ("The Church in the Wilderness".)

**RUDYARD LAKE**
The northern end of Rudyard Lake, about 1900. In the heyday of Rudyard as a pleasure resort steamers would transport passengers to the nearby golf course. This landing stage has now disappeared, nature having taken over to make the head of the lake a haven for water birds. In the background is the little station building of Cliffe Park Halt.

**RUDYARD LAKE, EARLY 1900s**

This is an extremely interesting social history item. The hand-propelled ice cream cart would be pushed by the vendor, Agostino Granelli. Leek and Macclesfield purveyors of ice cream often conveyed their wares to Rudyard by railway train - cart and all! Several members of the Granelli family came to this country independently around the turn of the century, setting up businesses in both Leek and Macclesfield, as well as other places. Some stayed only a short while before returning to their homeland, but there is to this day an ice cream manufacturer in Macclesfield by the name of Granelli.

**MEERBROOK VILLAGE,** c. 1905
Many changes took place in this picturesque village during the 1950s when some buildings were demolished before the land was submerged under the extended Tittesworth Reservoir. The above scene, however, is relatively unchanged, with the former endowed school on the left, the Three Horse Shoes straight ahead, and the former post office on the right.

**THE FOUNTAIN INN, MEERBROOK**
One of the many properties to be submerged under the enlarged Tittesworth Reservoir. This picture was taken in the 1950s, before the work commenced.

**HORSE-DRAWN SLEDGE, ABBEY GREEN,** c. 1900

This unusual spectacle of a horse-drawn sledge was taken outside the Abbey Farm, Abbey Green, Leek about 1900. Following the Dissolution of the Monasteries Dieulacres Abbey was sold to Sir Ralph Bagnall, and in 1597 passed to the Rudyerds who built this handsome half-timbered house close to the abbey ruins. The house bears the date 1612, and fragments from the abbey ruins were incorporated in some of the farm buildings.

**CHURCH STREET, LEEK,** c. 1905

St. Edward's Parish Church, Leek, showing the narrow Church Street, with carts by the churchyard wall. Elevated left is Clerk Bank, with Naylors Yard leading off. The shop with the sun blinds on the corner of Church Lane was Enoch Harrison, butcher. From here in 1902 a 10-year-old boy walked to Rudyard every Tuesday morning to take 2 lamb's fries and half lb. of lamb's liver to Tellwrights at Horton Lodge. He caught the 9 a.m. train back to Leek from Rudyard - the fare was 1d - and he ran all the way from Leek station to school in King Street, so as not to be late. For this, and additional work on Saturdays, he received one shilling per week.
On the right is Overton Bank, with Sampson Salt's builders yard.

**STOCKWELL STREET, LEEK,** c. 1913

Stockwell Street, Leek, showing in the background the copper dome of the Nicholson Institute (architects: Sugden & Son, completed 1884), in front of which stands Greystones, a 17th-century house which was the home of Mr. (later Sir) Arthur Nicholson, followed by Henry Salt. The large house nearer to the camera was Stockwell House, demolished in the 1930s to make way for New Stockwell House, opened by Sir Enoch Hill on 28th October 1937 to be the offices of the Leek and Moorland Building Society (now the Britannia Building Society) until their move to Newton House on Cheadle Road in 1970. Stockwell House was the home of Joshua Nicholson.

**FORD HOUSE, LEEK,** c. 1904
Ford House, corner of Market Street and Stockwell Street, Leek. Considered by many to be one of the most attractive houses in Leek, Ford House is now used as offices. Its name is believed to be derived from that of Hugh Ford (of the family of Fords of Ford Green Hall) and his wife Betty who moved to Leek around 1750 to occupy a brick farmhouse near the centre of the town, which at that time was surrounded by fields. They are thought to have built this 18th-century stone house which still bears their name.

**LEEK FROM ST. LUKE'S CHURCH TOWER,** c. 1910

In the distance, centre, is the square tower of St. Edward's Parish Church. To the left is the spire of the Congregational Church (now Trinity Church), whilst to the right stands the copper-domed Nicholson Insititute in Stockwell Street. A little nearer, the gable-end of the now-demolished Brunswick Methodist Church (Wesleyan) partially obscures the Town Hall (demolished 1988), both of which stood in Market Street. Nearer to the camera rises the squat but pointed tower of Bethesda Methodist Chapel (formerly New Connexion) which stood on the corner of Ball Haye Street and Queen Street (now a car park). On the right-hand edge, middle, can be seen part of the roof of the Regent Street Schoolroom, completed in 1880 for the Brunswick Methodists, and most recently in use as a Magistrates Court.

CATTLE MARKET LEEK.

**THE OLD CATTLE MARKET SITE, LEEK,** c. 1907
Taken by the photographer William Blake of Longton, this is a record of the area long before the Nicholson War Memorial became the focus of attention. St. Luke's Church is in the background, fronted by the shops in Cawdry Buildings (Fountain Street), and the Cattle Market Inn. Towards the right is the pointed spire of Fountain Street Primitive Methodist Chapel and Brough, Nicholson and Hall's factory and chimney (all now demolished). On the immediate right, part of the Talbot Hotel can be seen. The open space, where the three figures are walking, was known as Shude Hill between the wars, when it was set out with market stalls of all descriptions.

**DERBY STREET, LEEK, 1920s**
Hanley-Milton-Endon-Leek is the service operated by the P.M.T. bus on the left. The building on the right is the handsome Dutch-gabled swimming baths, now demolished. At the time, Derby Street had a cobbled road surface (setts), and the street lighting was mainly by gas-lamp.

**THE ANGEL, MARKET PLACE, LEEK**

The Angel formerly known as Platt's Vaults (now Yates' Wine Lodge). The building which has the date 1847 is one of the earliest examples of the work of the architect William Sugden, who (later with his son, Larner) was responsible for many of Leek's finest late-Victorian buildings.

**ST. EDWARD STREET, LEEK,** c. 1905

St. Edward Street, one of Leek's finest streets. Dr. Somerville's house and surgery (with the steps) is on the left. This was formerly the home of Andrew Jukes Worthington, founder of the textile company bearing his name. The building on the immediate right of the picture was the town house of Sir Thomas Wardle. The Elizabethan-style building towards the bottom of the street is Spout Hall, home of Hugh Sleigh, and the work of the architect Norman Shaw. The late Poet Laureate, Sir John Betjeman, enthused about the variegated architecture of St. Edward Street.

**SOUTHBANK STREET, LEEK,** 1905
Southbank Street, including the Post Office. This postcard, used on 2nd August 1905, reflects life in Edwardian Leek in one of the quieter streets of the town. The groups of people display the dress fashions of the day, and the deposits on the roadway remind us that the motor-car had not yet begun to dominate our lives.

**BUXTON ROAD, LEEK.**
This attractive snow scene shows, on the left, Waste Cottage, adjacent to which is The Waste, an area of trees and shrubs given to the town for recreational purposes by the local benefactor William Spooner Brough (1840-1917). On the right is the Moss Rose Inn and the road to Thorncliffe.

**LEEK AGRICULTURAL SHOW,** 7th-8th September, 1906
These scenes capture the spirit of the agricultural shows around the turn of the century - important and exciting events in the lives of the farming community. The gentleman with the white umbrella is Sir Arthur Nicholson, a highly respected and prominent member of the social and industrial scene.

**LEEK CEMETERY,** 1907

Graveside scene in Leek Cemetery on 18th July 1907. The occasion was the double funeral of two private soldiers in the 1st Volunteer Battalion of the North Staffordshire Regiment. James Bennett and John Bode, both of Leek, had drowned on 14th July (Bennett's 26th birthday) when their boat capsized on Rudyard Lake as they were returning from a visit to the Hanging Gate public house at Rushton. A third occupant of the boat, James Hill aged 23, had been rescued.

**LEEK PERSONALITIES, HIGH STREET,** c. 1910

Five Leek personalities pictured in High Street, outside Field House (now the National Reserve Club) L. to R. Jack Thurstan, a cardboard box manufacturer, with a factory in Leek. James Dunn, a native of Wellington (Salop), who travelled with Sir Philip Brocklehurst, Bart, on one of Shackleton's Antarctic expeditions, and remained with Sir Philip at Swythamley Hall. John Boughey, who kept the Golden Lion, formerly in Church Street, Leek. William Beresford, manager of the printing department in a local silk mill, proprietor of the Green Ball (off licence), Ball Haye Green, and a local bandsman. Isaac Carding, of the family of painters and plumbers, whose premises were in Leek Market Place. He, and several other members of his family, served with the Leek Fire Brigade.

**LEEK CORONATION CELEBRATIONS (KING GEORGE V),** 22nd June 1911
This scene shows the parade at the bottom of Ashbourne Road, with the banner of Ball Haye Green Wesleyan Sunday School prominent. For members of the parade, three names have been offered: leader of the left-hand column, a boy named Foster, leader of the right-hand column, Billy ("Widdy") Worthington, and another boy named Joe Sigley.

**GETLIFFE'S YARD, OFF DERBY STREET, LEEK,** c. 1920
A carnival day scene with 14 year-old George Smith astride the motor-cycle used to propel the carnival float of Arthur Hay and Sons, family grocers, of 57 Derby Street. White-bloused Mrs. Greenwood looks on approvingly from her doorway.

**DEDICATION OF THE NICHOLSON WAR MEMORIAL, LEEK,** 20th August 1925
Platform party (left to right): Col. Arthur Faulkner Nicholson (who presided); Sir Arthur Nicholson; the Bishop of Stafford; Lt. Gen. Sir Charles Harington; G. H. Wilson (Chairman, Leek Urban District Council); Gen. H. M. Clayton; Arthur Shaw (of Challinors and Shaw, solicitors); Lt. Col. Malcolm Nicholson; Capt. C. Kendall; Harold Henshaw (Town Clerk). Also present (although not seen in the picture) were Lady Nicholson; Rev. R. D. Jones; Rev. J. Ogmore Morgans; P. S. and S. H. Worthington (architects).

**ASHENHURST OLD MILL,** c. 1910
The old watermill at Ashenhurst, near Bradnop. In 1851 the miller was William Mountfort. The mill-house has been preserved, but little of the old mill remains, although parts of the mill race can still be traced. The nearby Ashenhurst Hall, home of the Phillips family for many years, was demolished in 1954.

**THORNCLIFFE BANK, Nr. LEEK,** c. 1906
A typical Moorland winter scene on Thorncliffe Bank, near Leek. The hardy nature of the Moorlanders is reflected by the two ladies with their pony. On the skyline is Clough House Farm and out-buildings. On the left is an interesting "scissors-stile". The road to the right is to Leek, passing Thorncliffe Chapel, which dates from 1839.

**ANCIENT ORDER OF FORESTERS MEETING,** c. 1910

Ancient Order of Foresters (Court No. 1427 Colliers' Refuge) meeting outside the New Inn, Upperhulme, about 1910. The licensee was John Thomas Wardle, and the inn is now "The Rock". The man astride the horse on the right is Alec Pickford of nearby Ferny Knowle Farm. The Ancient Order of Foresters was one of the many Friendly Societies formed following the Friendly Societies Act of 1896. They were flourishing at the time the photograph was taken, being the means by which working people, by contributing, could assure themselves of some income in times of need.

**LONGSDON POST OFFICE, c. 1910**
Why this picture was given the title of "The Market Place, Longsdon" is hard to understand. As far as the writer can discover no market has ever been held here. The scene is at the crossroads on the main Potteries-Leek road, with the road to Deep Haye Country Park off to the right. The building prominently featured is currently the village shop and post-office, although the post-office has been housed there only sporadically over the years.

**SUTHERLAND ROAD, LONGSDON,** c. 1925
The name of the road derives from the fact that the surrounding land was part of the estate of the Duke of Sutherland. The handsome stone-built house on the right is "The Firs" where Mr. "Road surveyor" Bailey used to live. At the time the photograph was taken it is believed to have been a small-holding owned by Mr. Phillips of J. Phillips (Ironmongers), Stockwell Street, Leek. The road continues out of sight over two canal bridges and a railway bridge at Wall Grange, and via the narrow Park Lane to Cheddleton.

Wall Grange.         V. L. Trafford, Leek.

## WALLGRANGE, c. 1910

From a vantage point either on the tow-path of the Caldon Canal on the Cheddleton side of Wallgrange railway station, or from the sloping woodland above it, this view of the Staffordshire Potteries Water Board pumping station was taken, nestling as it did beneath the embankment of the Leek arm of the Caldon Canal. On the skyline rises Mollats Wood, whilst in the foreground can be seen the Churnet Brook, dividing the Parish of Longsdon from that of Cheddleton. The postcard was published by the Leek photographer, V. L. Trafford.

**WATERFALL, WALLGRANGE,**
c. 1910

This waterfall was located at Wallgrange, near Longsdon, where the Potteries Waterworks Company, incorporated by Act of Parliament in 1847, had large supplies of fresh spring water discovered by their engineer Mr. L. Elliot.

**ST. LUKE'S (C. of E.) DAY SCHOOL, ENDON**

This picture, taken in Endon in the early 1900s, shows St. Luke's Church of England Day School, with the church lychgate in the background. The school was opened on Monday, 9th October 1871, surviving for 94 years before being demolished in 1965. The first headmaster, Mr. John Chadwick, stated in his report dated 13th October 1871: "The children are in a very backward state as they have only been able to attend dame schools: Three boys were tolerably well up ........ The Reverend James Badnall, vicar, very kindly assisted in the scripture lesson. The sewing has been voluntarily undertaken by the two ladies, Mrs. Badnall and Mrs. Smith".

**ENDON VILLAGE,** c. 1910
This view of the centre of the older part of Endon looks across the ford towards the well in the centre of the picture. The cottage on the left shows a brick-built extension over a much older stone-building. The building on the right, with the oval plaque, is the former Methodist Chapel. Built in 1835 at a cost of £217 it had seating for 110 people. A Sunday School was also held. This chapel closed when the new Methodist chapel on the main road near the 'Fountain' was opened in 1876. It was later converted to the cottages as seen in the picture.

**ENDON VILLAGE AFTER THE FLOODS,** 1927
Virtually the same view as the previous page showing the devastation following the disastrous floods of 1927.

**ENDON VILLAGE**

This view, looking towards the road to Gratton, shows the village well, erected in 1845 by a local landowner, Thomas Heaton. It was presented to the village on 29th May 1845, when a number of local tradesmen and other villagers created a spontaneous celebration by dressing the well with oakleaves (a connection with the ancient Oak Apple Day traditions) and other flowers. This "well-dressing" has been perpetuated annually ever since, on the same weekend, which is now the Spring Bank Holiday.

**ENDON WELL-DRESSING,** 1912

These industrious well-dressers, together with all their accoutrements are believed to be from left to right: Thomas Gratton; William Pickford; Noah Baddeley (village cobbler); Jack Stubbs. The spectator is Rev. John Simon Morris, the vicar who would play an important role at the Well-dressing ceremony. The Well-dressing Queen in 1912 was Miss R. Broomfield. There is no longer a shop next to the well at Spring Cottage (to the right) - in 1912 it was owned by Robert Irwin, grocer and general dealer.

**ENDON WELL-DRESSING,** 1927

One of the traditions of the well-dressing ceremony at Endon is the offering of a glass of water from the well to the Well-dressing Queen by the vicar. In this scene young Miss Sally Simcock has received the blessed water from the hand of the Rev. John Simon Morris. Afterwards, on the nearby Jaw Bone Field, there is "all the fun of the fair", with May-pole dancing, side shows, roundabouts, swing-boats, refreshments and sports.

**THE BIG FLOOD AT ENDON,** 1914

Although the Endon flood of 12th July 1927 was comprehensively reported in the newspapers of the day, little seems to be known about a quite devastating flood which occured in August 1914. (Perhaps it was overshadowed by the imminence of war). Generations of Endonians have experienced flooding of the low-lying area of their parish, so that until recent remedial work was carried out, the event was forseen as an almost inevitable annual occurance.

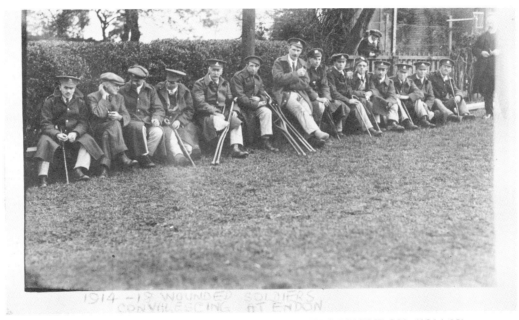

**CONVALESCENT WAR WOUNDED SOLDIERS AT ENDON,** (1914-18)
This not-so-joyous scene is something of a departure from the usual high-spirited festivities which take place on this site - the Jaw Bone Field - at the time of the well-dressing festival.

**STAFFORD ARMS, BAGNALL,** early 1920s
The inn, said to have been built about 1400, of local sandstone, stands in the centre of the village. Stables were added about 100 years later, and in 1815 mullioned windows were inserted. The inn has associations with Bonnie Prince Charlie, one of the rooms being thought to have been used as an armoury. John Sleigh, in his book "A history of the ancient parish of Leek", suggests that the Prince stayed at Bagnall Hall on his retreat from Derby in 1745. He states: "About 30 of their horses came to Bagnall, and took Justice Murhall along with them, and kept him 2 or 3 days: it's said he gave 'em £300 to be released".

**THE BROOK, LEEKBROOK**
The brook at Leekbrook, which marked the traditional boundary between Cheddleton and Leek. The main road to Leek passes under the railway bridge on the left of the picture. Much of this area is now part of the industrial estate.

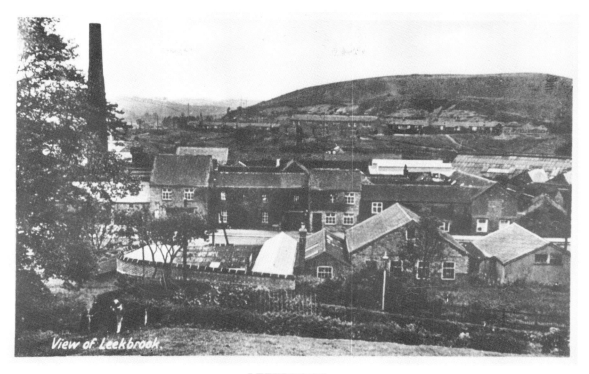

## LEEKBROOK
This view of Leekbrook overlooks Joshua Wardle's old works, with the row of Railway Cottages and the railway line in the background. Also in the picture, alongside the road to the right, is the old Traveller's Rest.

## LEEKBROOK
The Leekbrook War Memorial takes the unusual form of a rough stone block with a flagpole a few feet behind. The plaque commemorating the Great War 1914-1918, with the names of 10 local men and their regiments, is affixed to the flagpole.

## THE CHEDDLETON FLINT MILLS

There exists a record of a water mill in Cheddleton as early as 1253, and in 1580 two mills - one a fulling mill and the other a corn mill. Ralph Wood was a miller in the 1720s, and the Wood family became prominent pottery manufacturers in Burslem.

The North Mill was built to grind flint for the pottery industry in about 1770, and is characteristic of the work of James Brindley.

Old Photograph of Cheddleton Flint Mill

**CHEDDLETON VILLAGE,** c. 1906
This picture of the main road through Cheddleton shows the Red Lion on the right, and was taken before the level of the road was raised, about 1930. When this work was done the horse troughs on the left and the mounting block on the right were removed.

**CHEDDLETON VILLAGE, c. 1910**
A view of the old part of Cheddleton village, looking from the direction of the village green and the area known as "London Bridge" towards the top of Hollow Lane. On the left is the church lychgate, in beautifully carved stone, presented by Mrs. Bradshaw in memory of her late husband, the Rev. Samuel Bradshaw.

## CHEDDLETON BRIDGE

A view of Cheddleton looking across the River Churnet, with the road bridge on the right. The large building on the left (now the Flintlock) was the birthplace on 2 October 1803 of Richard Cooper, who became a member of the Royal College of Surgeons, Medical Officer to the Leekfrith District of Leek Union 1836-1871, and a lifelong Methodist. The building was also once known as "The Bridge" or "Wharf Inn".

**CHEDDLETON RAILWAY STATION**, c. 1910
Cheddleton Railway Station, on the Churnet Valley line of the North Staffordshire Railway which ran from North Rode to Rocester, opened 13 July 1849. Attributed by Sir John Betjeman to the architect A. W. N. Pugin, the building work was supervised by William Sugden, architect, of Leek. The line was closed in 1960, and the station buildings have been preserved by the (new) North Staffordshire Railway Company as a museum.

**CHEDDLETON VILLAGE**, c. 1910
In the middle distance, centre, of this view of Cheddleton are the 3 silk weavers cottages on Station Road, demolished in 1980. In front of these was the site of the late 18th-century tanyard. The building to the right of the cottages was formerly the Railway Hotel. The large building on the left is the old Churnet Hall, used for entertainments for a time. A trade directory of 1932 lists: Churnet Cinema (Rev. W. G. Burgis). Near to this was the old Cheddleton Brewery, closed in 1915. Amongst the family names involved in the brewery were those of Kent, Smith (related to the Joules of Stone) and Illsley.

**WETLEY ROCKS**
Wetley Rocks village, the main road, about 1905. The notice board behind the wall on the left marks the site of the old Methodist Chapel. In the centre of the picture, hidden by the horse and cart, was the old wheelwright's yard.

**WETLEY ROCKS**
The inn on the right is the Powys Arms, formerly The Arblasters' Arms. The inn thus commemorates the family names of former Lords of the Manor of Cheddleton - the Arblasters of Rownall Hall held the lordship from about 1620 to 1787, when it passed by marriage to the Powys family of Shrewsbury. There is another inn in the picture - the Mason's Arms which stood on the left-hand side of the road, in the shadow of the rocks, on the site of the present petrol filling station.

**THE CHURNET VALLEY,** c. 1912

The Churnet Valley, near Consall, showing the two forms of transport - railway and canal-side by side. The Caldon Canal was opened in 1777, its prime purpose being the transportation of limestone from the Caldon Low quarries to the Potteries, where it joined the Trent and Mersey Canal at Etruria. The engineer was James Brindley. The Churnet Valley Railway opened in 1849, and its greater speed and carrying capacity spelt the end of the canal.

**THE CHURNET VALLEY**
The river-canal near Consall in the Churnet Valley. In this very narrow part of the valley the builders of the Caldon Canal found it necessary to utilise the actual course of the River Churnet itself, so, for a distance of about a mile, from Oakmeadow Ford Lock, south of Cheddleton, to Consall Forge the river and canal share the same bed.

**CONSALL FORGE, THE CHURNET VALLEY**
In the heart of the Churnet Valley, at Consall Forge, the river and canal divide, to follow their separate courses again. Consall Forge was the site of a 17th-century iron working site. There were also limekilns and a water mill nearby.

**FROGHALL STATION**
Froghall Station - also serving Kingsley - on the Churnet Valley line of the North Staffordshire Railway. The station was closed for passengers on 7 November 1960, and for goods on 4 May 1964. The A52 road bridge is in the background.

**FROGHALL WHARF**

Froghall Wharf - the terminus of the Caldon Canal. Here the waggons bringing the limestone from Caldon Low Quarries were unloaded, and the stone transferred to canal boats, or burned in the huge limekilns. The transportation system from the quarries to Froghall was a series of tramways or industrial railways - the first being laid in 1779, re-aligned 1783. This was followed by John Rennie's 1802 line, and finally the more direct 1849 line. The waggons were usually pulled by horses, but later winding drums helped to winch the waggons up the inclines on their journey to and from the quarries 3.5 miles away and 600 feet higher, the return being by gravity.

**CAULDON VILLAGE, NEAR WATERHOUSES**, c. 1905
The Church of St. Mary and St. Lawrence dates mainly from 1781-1784, although some parts are earlier. The quarries at nearby Caldon Low have dominated the economy of the area for over 200 years, and, together with farming, have provided much employment for the residents, many of whom lived in the sturdy cottages built with local stone.

**THE QUARRIES, CALDON LOW, NEAR WATERHOUSES,** c. 1908
In 1769 the proprietors of the Trent and Mersey Canal took out a 999-year lease on the large area of carboniferous limestone around Caldon Low. Quarrying began, and in 1776 the Caldon Canal was authorised - its main purpose being to transport the limestone from Caldon Low via Froghall to Etruria in Stoke-on-Trent. The stone was transported from the quarries to the canal basin at Froghall by a series of industrial tramways. Some of the lines and waggons at the quarry site are seen in this picture.

**INTERIOR OF CALDON LOW CAVE,** c. 1910
This North Staffordshire Railway postcard shows the interior of a cave in the limestone at Caldon Low that was discovered during quarrying operations. The cave was 30 feet wide, 100 feet high and penetrated about 140 feet into the hill. It is probable that at one time the cavity was an underground watercourse.

**WATERHOUSES,** c. 1904

The Straker Steam Bus at Waterhouses in 1904. Two such buses were owned by the North Staffordshire Railway. They were built by Strakers of Bristol, and were 35 horse power fired by coke, and weighed 2 tons and 19 cwts when empty. They were somewhat unreliable (one broke down on the opening day) and uncomfortable. The iron wheels caused great vibration, and shop-window displays in Leek collapsed as they passed by - this led to the banning of the buses in Leek's main streets. The service ran from Leek Station to Waterhouses, and closed on 5th June 1905.

**WATERHOUSES**
A view of Waterhouses village about 1905, just after the Leek and Manifold Valley Light Railway was opened, taken from the site of the station. The old village school, which still has its bell and bell turret intact, is to the left of the white building (Ye Olde Crown Hotel), half hidden by the tree. The large building in the centre of the picture is the now-extended and enlarged general store and post office.

**WATERHOUSES**, c. 1905
This view of Waterhouses shows the main Ashbourne road through the village before the road was widened. The old stone bridge over the River Hamps on the right carries the narrow road via Lea House to Waterfall. The building on the left is Ye Olde Crown Hotel.

**THE RIVER HAMPS AT FORD**
This rather dramatic view of the river in spate is typical of Nithsdale's pictures - he had a true photographer's eye for the unusual viewpoint.

**SPARROWLEE STATION**

Sparrowlee Station, on the Leek and Manifold Valley Light Railway, was the first stop beyond Waterhouses. The sender of this postcard, sent 25 October 1904, has added his own comment alongside the picture. Sparrowlee served about six farms in the vicinity, and was the nearest station for Waterfall.

**REDHURST,** c. 1910
Redhurst, Manifold Valley, with a train going south. At Redhurst, $5^{1}/_{4}$ miles from Waterhouses, the line crossed the River Manifold. The station had a small platform and milkstand, and was another stop for Wetton.

**THOR'S CAVE,
MANIFOLD VALLEY,** c. 1929
Thor's Cave, $4^3/_4$ miles from Waterhouses. In the days of the Leek and Manifold Valley Light Railway there was a platform and shelter, and until 1917 a refreshment room. A popular stopping place for tourists, the cave was always a great attraction, as it still is today. The huge cliff rises 350 feet above the valley, and the cave is 23 feet wide and 35 feet high, rising to 60 feet inside. (The sender of this postcard, used in 1929, describes the train as " a funny, fussy little thing").

THORS CAVE, MANIFOLD VALLEY

THE MANIFOLD VALLEY RAILWAY TRAIN.

**THE MANIFOLD VALLEY RAILWAY,** c. 1908

The two Manifold Valley locomotives were named "E.R. Calthrop" (pictured here) and "J.B. Earle", thus commemorating the names of the Engineer and Resident Engineer respectively. They were built by Kitson and Co at a cost of £1,725 each, and were the first 2-6-4 tank engines to run in Great Britain.

**THE MANIFOLD VALLEY RAILWAY, HULME END**
This North Staffordshire Railway postcard shows the Manifold Valley locomotive "E.R. Calthrop" at Hulme End, $8\frac{1}{4}$ miles from Waterhouses. The track in the foreground is the run-round loop to the loco shed, and the track to the carriage shed. On the other side of the platform were two standard gauge sidings in the goods yard. This photograph was taken on the opening day of the Leek and Manifold Valley Light Railway, Monday 27 June 1904. The date had originally been fixed for Whit Monday, 23 May, but late delivery of the engines and some of the coaches led to a postponement.

**WETTON MILL, MANIFOLD VALLEY,** c. 1920s

Wetton Mill, in the heart of the Manifold Valley. Now a popular gathering point for hikers, cyclists and campers, but in the days of the light railway it was rather isolated. Its station, an open platform and milk stand, served Wetton village about a mile away, uphill. The fact that most of the villages served by the Leek and Manifold Valley Light Railway were some distance from the line, usually with a steep climb out of the valley, was another factor in the demise of the railway.

**ECTON COPPER MINES,** c. 1910
Early mining activities were taking place around Ecton in the 17th century, but the greatest period of expansion and prosperity occured when the ownership of the mines passed to successive Dukes of Devonshire. The first lease of 1723 was not successful, and in 1739 a new lease was granted to the 3rd Duke of Devonshire, John Gilbert-Cooper of Spondon and others. In 1760 the 4th Duke decided to work the mines on his own account, and between 1760 and 1768 5,862 tons of ore were produced. Production rose enormously between 1776 and 1817 when 55,857 tons of ore were produced showing a profit of £244,734 (about £6000 per year). The Duke ceased operating in 1825, and there followed a period of decline. New companies came and went, but by 1887 all was virtually finished.

**ECTON,** c. 1912

At Ecton, 7¼ miles from Waterhouses, the valley opens out and was, in the past, heavily industrialised. In addition to the copper mines there was a creamery served by a siding and built on the site of an old smelting house. This provided much of the commercial traffic for the light railway in its latter days with a direct milk tanker service from Ecton to Finsbury Park every night. Alas the creamery closed in 1932 and with the mines being long abandoned the demise of the light railway was inevitable. The last train ran on Saturday, 10th March 1934.

**ECTON LEA**
A peaceful rural scene at Ecton Lea in the Manifold Valley. There was a refreshment room at Ecton Lea in the days of the Leek and Manifold Valley Light Railway.

**HULME END STATION**
The Leek and Manifold Valley Light Railway train at Hulme End - the terminus of the line. There was a loco shed here, and a siding led into a carriage shed. Tickets (see insert) could be bought from the booking office here and at Waterhouses. At other halts along the line tickets would be issued on the train, by the Bell Punch method.

**HULME END**
A view of the village, circa 1930. The building in the middle of the picture is advertising "Refreshments", for this was in the days of the Leek and Manifold Valley Light Railway.

Sheen

## SHEEN

This picture reflects the rural nature of Sheen in the early 1900s. Sheen is situated on a ridge above the River Manifold, near to the Staffordshire/Derbyshire border. Close by is Sheen Hill, a 1247ft-high peak. Although not in this photograph, Sheen has an interesting 15th-century village cross and an ancient burial ground known as the Royal Low. Its church, St. Luke's, was rebuilt in 1850, and its large Victorian parsonage is a splendid example of the work of the architect Butterfield (1852).

**THE BLACK LION, BUTTERTON,** c. 1905
It was not unusual at the time this photograph was taken for licensees to follow the joint occupations of inn-keeper and smallholder, in fact, it was almost the custom. Tom Bateman, landlord of the Black Lion at Butterton, was no exception. He is seen here, extreme left, with his family: Mary Ann Bateman (wife), daughters Mable (Mrs. Rudge), Sarah (Mrs. Mathews), Kate (Mrs. Upton) and son-in-law Harold Upton. Tom Bateman later moved to Leek to become landlord of the Dog and Partridge and then the Black's Head, both in Leek's main thoroughfare.

**THE CROSS-ROADS, BUTTERTON**
Butterton was strategically placed on the old packhorse route in the days when copper was conveyed by horse and cart from the mines at Ecton to the smelting works at Whiston. The church at Butterton is Victorian (1871), with its spire by the Leek architect, Sugden (1879).

The School, Alstonfield

**THE SCHOOL, ALSTONFIELD,** c. 1905
A school was established in Alstonfield in 1828 as a result of a donation of £5 and 30 acres of land from the Harpur-Crewe family in 1820, to launch the project. The remainder of the money was raised by public subscription. The school was opened in 1842. The conveyance of the site by Sir George Crewe to Rev. John Simpson, Richard B. Manclarke, Daniel Cantrell, James Hambleton and William Mellor is dated 4th May 1842. An extension was completed in 1895 at a cost of £337-6-10, with a further enlargement later. The school closed in 1982.

The Chapel and Smithy, Alstonefield

## THE CHAPEL AND SMITHY, ALSTONFIELD, c. 1905

This charming village was at one time the centre of a much larger community. Lying between the rivers Dove and Manifold the parish embraced, in 1834, Elkstones, Fawfieldhead, Heathylee, Hollinsclough, Longnor, Quarnford and Warslow, amongst others. Today many of the cottages display "Bed and Breakfast" signs, but the village remains unspoiled. The Wesleyan Chapel, built in 1824, formerly in the old Wetton and Longnor circuit of the Methodist Church, closed in 1981, and is now a private house and joinery workshop.

**ALSTONFIELD VILLAGE,** c. 1908

This photograph shows the post office and tea-shop on the right. Several mullioned-windowed houses, just out of sight, form a delightful group with the George Inn around the village green, between which and the church is the Hall, formerly the rectory, rebuilt by the Harpurs of Swarkestone and Calke in 1587 and renamed "The Hall". Behind this is a tithe-barn featuring an internal wall of exposed wattle and daub and a spiral stone staircase, both probably part of the original rectory.

## HOLLINSCLOUGH

This isolated Moorland village is situated in the Upper Dove Valley, in the shadow of Chrome and Parkhouse hills. The rather odd Church of St. Agnes (1840) is on the right of the picture. The church has a two-storeyed porch, and a house is built on to the west end. The bell turret is also unusual. The church is now a residential centre for the Frank Wheldon School, Carlton, Nottingham. The building on the left is Vicarage Cottage, to the left of which (out of the picture) is the Methodist Chapel (1801).

## THE "CHESHIRE CHEESE", LONGNOR

"The Township of Longnor" is the true name for this gritty Moorland village, for in bygone days it was an important market centre for the area. In the churchyard is the grave of William Billinge, who, according to his tombstone, died within a few yards of the cornfield at Fawfieldhead in which he was born in 1679, 112 years later in 1791, having soldiered around the world, including serving under the Duke of Marlborough at the Battle of Ramillies on 23rd May 1706. This interesting group of fashionable ladies was photographed outside the "Cheshire Cheese" which displays an inn sign in the form of a whole cheese.

**TOWN HEAD, LONGNOR,** early 1900s
This pastoral scene reflects the nature of this moorland farming community. Longnor was designated a Conservation Area in 1977, and the Peak District National Park has done much to halt the rural decay which was threatening so much of its livelihood, by encouraging the controlled growth of small industries.

**LONGNOR**
Another picture of Longnor in the early 1900s, which shows its sloping cobbled market place, overlooked by substantial buildings of local stone. In the centre is the Market Hall (1873) with its arched entrance, over which is the market toll board displaying charges for various animals - a reminder that in bygone days members of the farming community would gather here to present their stock for sale.

**LONGNOR**
The rural nature of Longnor is captured in this village scene, so typical of the high moorland area whose people are a hardy race. This fact is typified by the following death notice published in the Westminster Magazine of 1780: "LONGNOR, NEAR BUXTON, DERBYSHIRE, Samuel Fidler, aged 105. He walked from his own house to Buxton within three days of his death, which is upwards of five miles".

**WARSLOW POST OFFICE,** c. 1900
The village has a typical Peak District character and many fine stone buildings similar to those shown here. The post office was kept by S. Belfield, who was also a grocer, draper and provision dealer. A 1928 trade directory reveals that a Belfield was still keeping the post office at that time. Warslow church, built in 1820, has some fine Pre-Raphaelite glass in the chancel windows.

**WARSLOW VILLAGE,** c. 1906
This picture of Warslow village shows a group of children playing a game on the open space in front of the Greyhound Inn. The auctioneer's notice on the small hoarding announces that Fergyson and Son will conduct a sale of antiques, china and furniture at The Brund, Sheen.

**FLASH,** c. 1910

On the left, with horse-drawn vehicles outside, is the New Inn, reputed to be the highest licensed house in England. In the centre, with the double flight of stone steps, is the chapel. There was a strong society of Methodists at Flash as early as 1773, at the height of the ministry of John Wesley. The chapel, built in 1784, was visited by Wesley, and is one of the oldest chapels in the district, although it is now closed for worship. A novel set in and around Flash was written by Judge Ruegg, K.C. and published in 1928.

**LOWE HILL BRIDGE**
The old Lowe Hill bridge over the main Leek to Ashbourne road, viewed from the Leek side. The bridge was the scene of many road accidents, being too low and narrow for modern traffic, and has now been replaced by a modern bridge.

**ST. LEONARD'S CHURCH, IPSTONES,** c. 1911
This late 18th-century church was generously endowed by John Sneyd of Belmont Hall, and contains several memorials to members of the Sneyd family - Jane Sneyd 1840, William Debank Sneyd 1825 and Ralph Sneyd 1821. The chancel dating from 1902, was designed by Gerald Horsley.

**IPSTONES**

Another Moorlands village scene from yesteryear, captured for the series of postcards produced by G. Hill and Sons. This is the main road through Ipstones, looking north towards the toll-house. Considerable modern housing development has taken place on the left-hand side, but the cottages on the right are largely unaltered.

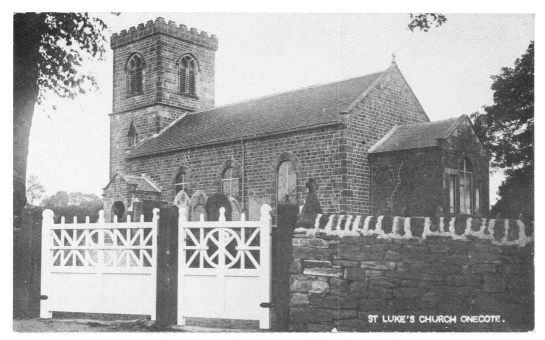

**ST. LUKE'S CHURCH, ONECOTE,** c. 1908
St. Luke's Church, Onecote, was built in 1753-5. The low, short chancel appears to be out of proportion to the nave, and the Venetian east window is very plain. The west tower is short but imposing. The name of the village literally means One Cot (i.e. cottage).

**ST. LUKE'S CHURCH, ONECOTE**
The well-proportioned nave is lit by six arched windows. The simple style is typical of many Anglican churches in the Moorland area. The church is built on the site of a much earlier one.

**PARADISE WALK, Nr. ILAM HALL,** c. 1920s

This idyllic, pastoral scene shows the entrance to the Paradise Walk, just below Ilam Hall. Along this stretch the River Manifold can be seen bubbling up out of its underground course. This Peak District phenomenon occurs during dry weather, when the River Manifold disappears underground near Wetton Mill, to follow its subterranean course to this point.

**ILAM CHURCH,** c. 1930

The Church of the Holy Cross, Ilam, is basically medieval, but was greatly restored by Gilbert Scott in 1855-6. Although the church is dominated by the Watts Russell Memorial there are many other interesting features. The chapel on the south side dates from 1618. The font is Norman. The blocked doorway on the south side is probably Saxon. The ornate wrought iron screens are the work of Scott, as is also the north arcade. In the churchyard stand two fine late Anglo-Saxon crosses, of the type usually found in the Peak District.

Ilam Hall, Staffordshire

## ILAM HALL

This imposing building, with its battlements and turrets, was the home of the Watts Russell family. Rebuilt in 1821 by Jesse Watts Russell, the architect was John Shaw the elder. Much of the hall was demolished in 1934, the remaining buildings being converted to a youth hostel.

**ILAM,** c. 1910

This composite postcard shows many of the features of Ilam that are often neglected by the visitor who passes quickly through the village on his way to Dovedale. The Watts Russell memorial chapel by Chantrey was erected in 1831 in memory of David Pike Watts and forms an octagonal extension to the church. The cross at the end of the village street, near the river bridge, is in memory of the first Mrs. Watts Russell and was erected by her husband in 1840, to the design of Gilbert Scott.

**THE FISHING TEMPLE BERESFORD DALE,** c. 1910

The Fishing Temple, Beresford Dale, is Charles Cotton's old house restored. Over the door the initials of Isaac Walton and Charles Cotton form a monogram. Above them is the dedication: PISCATORIBUS SACRUM 1674. Two famous Staffordshire men, Walton was born at Stafford in 1593 and Cotton at Beresford about 1630. To quote "Viator" in "Compleat Angler": "I am most pleased with this little house of anything I ever saw. It stands in a kind of peninsular, too, with a delicate, clear river about...... fine lights, finely wainscotted, and all exceedingly neat, with a marble table and all in the middle".

(There is no public access).

Fishing Hut, Beresford Dale

119

**DOVEDALE,** c. 1906
Frequently associated with the Derbyshire Peak District, Dovedale is more correctly Staffordshire, for at this point the River Dove forms the boundary between the two counties. A long-time favourite with visitors and hikers, endless delightful riverside scenes await the true walker who is prepared to venture along the dale beyond the famous stepping stones.
These Edwardian scenes show typical crowds of visitors in Dovedale.

# ACKNOWLEDGEMENTS

The authors wish to thank the following for their help in preparing this publication:
Robert Milner for advice on the Cheddleton section
Colin McLean for the loan of postcards of Biddulph
The staff of Leek Library
Steve Benz for his encouragement and advice on publication.

The following publications have been consulted:
History of the Ancient Parish of Leek - John Sleigh
Olde Leeke - M. H. Miller (Vols. 1 and 2)
The Sugdens of Leek - G. A. Lovenbury
The Building of England: Staffordshire - N. Pevsner
Cheddleton: a village history, ed. R. Milner
Biddulph ("By the Diggings"), ed. J. Kennedy
Biddulph Grange - Anne Ferris
Peakland Roads and Trackways - A. E. and E. M. Dodd
The Leek and Manifold Valley Light Railway - "Manifold"
The Copper and Lead Mines of Ecton Hill - J. A. Robey and L. Porter
Alstonefield: a village history - Alstonefield Local History Society
Dane Valley Story - C. Rathbone
The Old Road to Endon, ed. R. Speake
White's Directory of Staffordshire (1851)
Various trade directories of Staffordshire

Finally, a word of acknowledgement to the many publishers, local and national, of topographical picture postcards, whose efforts in the past have done much to preserve images of bygone days in the Staffordshire Moorlands. For our part, we are grateful for this opportunity to perpetuate their fine work.

Also published by Brampton Publications in the series "A Portrait in Old Picture Postcards":

Potteries Picture Postcards; A Portrait of the Six Towns
Potteries Picture Postcards, Volume 2; A Second Portrait of the Six Towns
Potteries Picture Postcards, Volume 3; A Third Portrait of the Six Towns
Trentham and Tittensor
Kidsgrove, Talke and Mow Cop
Stone, Sandon and Barlaston
The Borough of Newcastle-under-Lyme
Eccleshall and District
The Staffordshire Moorlands, Volume 1
Ashley, Loggerheads and Woore

Congleton and District
Crewe
Nantwich, Worleston and Wybunbury

Market Drayton and Norton-in-Hales

R.M.S. "Titanic"

Other local titles in preparation, for details write to Brampton Publications.